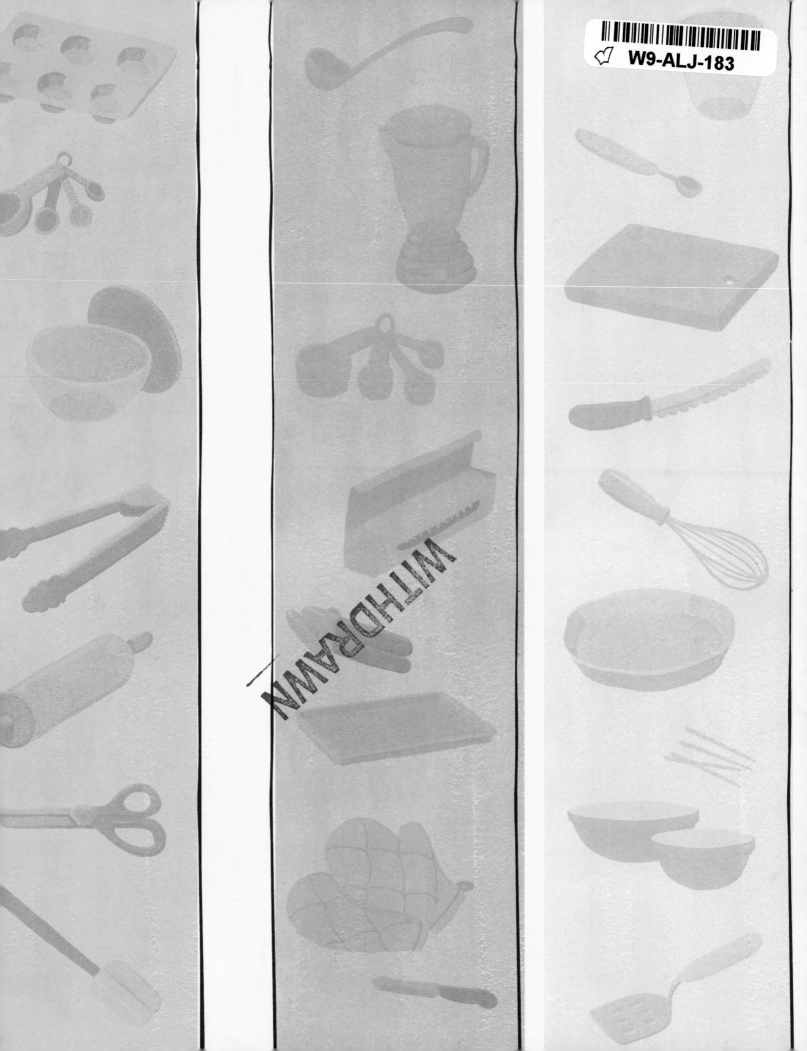

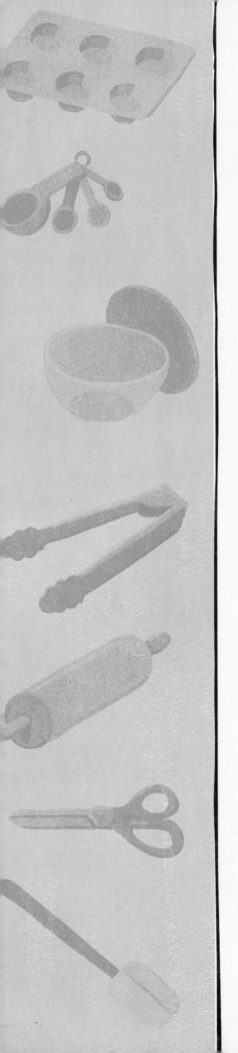
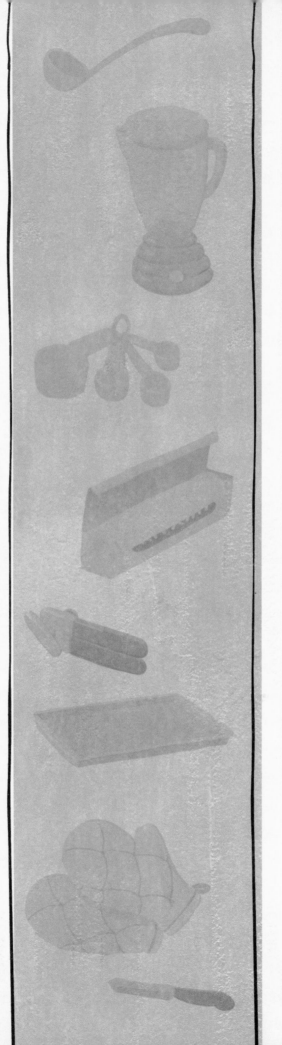

Puffy Popovers

and Other
Get-Out-of-Bed Breakfasts

by Nick Fauchald   illustrated by Rick Peterson

Special thanks to our content adviser:
Joanne L. Slavin, Ph.D, R.D.
Professor of Food Science and Nutrition
University of Minnesota

PICTURE WINDOW BOOKS
Minneapolis, Minnesota

Editors: Christianne Jones and Carol Jones
Designer: Tracy Davies
Page Production: Melissa Kes

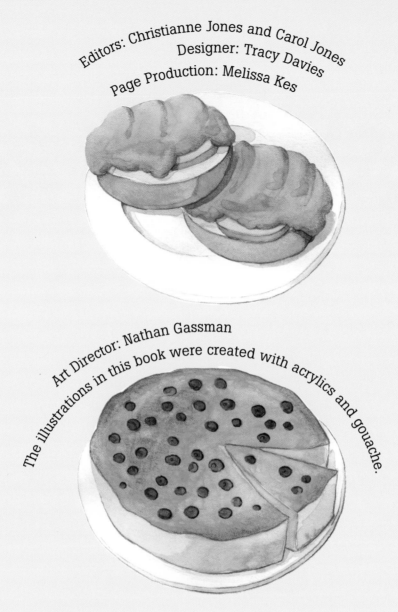

Art Director: Nathan Gassman
The illustrations in this book were created with acrylics and gouache.

The illustration on page 5 is from *www.mypyramid.gov.*

Printed in the United States of America

All books published by Picture Window Books are manufactured with paper containing at least 10 percent post-consumer waste.

Library of Congress Cataloging-in-Publication Data
Fauchald, Nick.
Puffy popovers : and other get-out-of-bed breakfasts / by Nick Fauchald ; illustrated by Rick Peterson.
p. cm. — (Kids dish)
Includes index.
ISBN-13: 978-1-4048-3996-0 (library binding)
1. Breakfasts—Juvenile literature. I. Peterson, Rick. II. Title.
TX733.F387 2008
641.5'2—dc22   2007032924

Editors' note: The author based the difficulty levels of the recipes on the skills and time required, as well as the number of ingredients and tools needed. Adult help and supervision is required for all recipes.

Table of Contents

EASY

INTERMEDIATE

ADVANCED

Nick Fauchald is the author of many children's books. After attending the French Culinary School in Manhattan, he helped launch the magazine *Every Day with Rachael Ray*. He is currently an editor at *Food & Wine* magazine and lives in New York City. Although Nick has worked with some of the world's best chefs, he still thinks kids are the most fun and creative cooks to work with.

Dear Kids,

A healthy breakfast helps jump-start your day. It supplies the energy needed to learn and play. The recipes in this book were made especially for beginning cooks like you.

Cooking is fun, and safety in the kitchen is very important. As you begin your cooking adventure, please remember these tips:

★ Make sure an adult is in the kitchen with you.
★ Tie back your hair and tuck in all loose clothing.
★ Read the recipe from start to finish before you begin.
★ Wash your hands before you start and whenever they get messy.
★ Wash all fresh fruits and vegetables.
★ Take your time cutting the ingredients.
★ Use oven mitts whenever you are working with hot foods or equipment.
★ Stay in the kitchen the entire time you are cooking.
★ Clean up when you are finished.

Now, choose a recipe that sounds tasty, check with an adult, and get cooking. Your friends and family are hungry!

Enjoy,
Nick

Note to Adults:

Learning to cook is an exciting, challenging adventure for young people. It helps kids build confidence, learn responsibility, become familiar with food and nutrition, practice math, science, and motor skills, and follow directions. Here are some ways you can help kids get the most out of their cooking experiences:

• Encourage them to read the entire recipe before they begin cooking. Make sure they have everything they need and understand all of the steps.

• Make sure young cooks have a kid-friendly workspace. If your kitchen counter is too high for them, offer them a stepstool or a table to work at.

• Expect new cooks to make a little mess, and encourage them to clean it up when they are finished.

• Help multiple cooks divide the tasks before they begin.

• Enjoy what the kids just cooked together.

MyPyramid

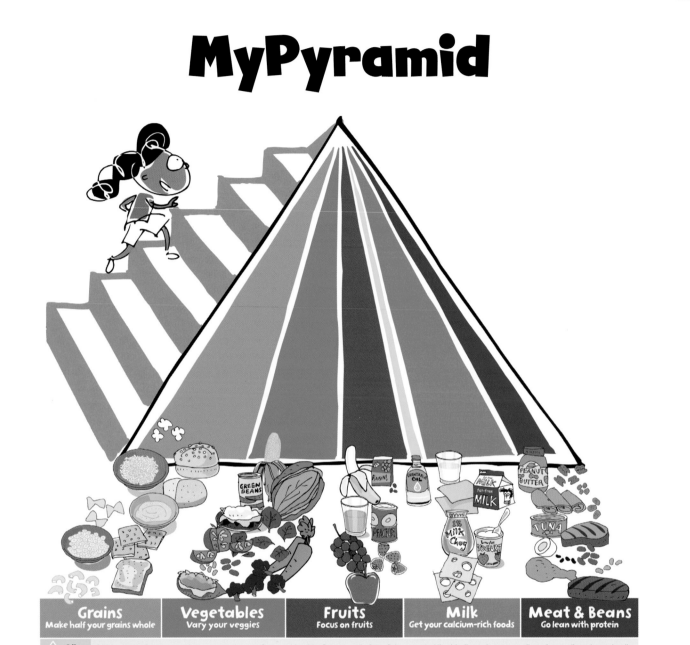

| **Grains**
Make half your grains whole | **Vegetables**
Vary your veggies | **Fruits**
Focus on fruits | **Milk**
Get your calcium-rich foods | **Meat & Beans**
Go lean with protein |

💧 **Oils**   Oils are not a food group, but you need some for good health. Get your oils from fish, nuts, and liquid oils such as corn oil, soybean oil, and canola oil.

In 2005, the U.S. government created MyPyramid, a plan for healthful eating and living. The new MyPyramid plan contains 12 separate diet plans based on your age, gender, and activity level. For more information about MyPyramid, visit *www.mypyramid.gov.*

The pyramid at the top of each recipe shows the main food groups included. Use the index to find recipes that include food from the food group of your choice, major ingredients used, recipe levels, and appliances/equipment needed.

Special Tips and Glossary

Cracking Eggs: Tap the egg on the counter until it cracks. Hold the egg over a small bowl. Gently pull the two halves of the shell apart until the contents fall into the bowl.

Measuring Dry Ingredients: Measure dry ingredients (such as flour and sugar) by spooning the ingredient into a measuring cup until it's full. Then level off the top of the cup with the back of a butter knife.

Measuring Wet Ingredients: Place a clear measuring cup on a flat surface, then pour the liquid into the cup until it reaches the correct measuring line. Be sure to check the liquid at eye level.

Bake: cook food in an oven

Cool: set hot food on a wire rack until it's no longer hot

Cover: place container lid, plastic wrap, or aluminum foil over a food; use aluminum foil if you're baking the food, and plastic wrap if you're chilling, freezing, microwaving, or leaving it on the counter

Drizzle: to lightly pour

Flip: turn a piece of food over

Grease: spread butter, cooking spray, or shortening on a piece of cookware so food doesn't stick

Melt: heat a solid (such as butter) until it becomes a liquid

Preheat: turn an oven on before you use it; it usually takes about 15 minutes to preheat an oven

Slice: cut something into thin pieces

Sprinkle: to scatter something in small bits

Stir: mix ingredients with a spoon until blended

Whisk: stir a mixture rapidly until it's smooth

METRIC CONVERSION CHART

1/2 teaspoon (2.5 milliliters)
3/4 teaspoon (3 milliliters)
1 teaspoon (5 milliliters)
2 teaspoons (10 milliliters)

1 tablespoon (15 milliliters)
2 tablespoons (30 milliliters)
3 tablespoons (45 milliliters)
4 tablespoons (60 milliliters)

1/8 cup (30 milliliters)
1/4 cup (60 milliliters)
1/3 cup (75 milliliters)
1/2 cup (125 milliliters)
2/3 cup (150 milliliters)
3/4 cup (180 milliliters)

1 cup (250 milliliters)
1 1/4 cups (300 milliliters)
1 1/2 cups (375 milliliters)
2 cups (500 milliliters)
3 cups (750 milliliters)

TEMPERATURE CONVERSION CHART

325° Fahrenheit (165° Celsius)
350° Fahrenheit (175° Celsius)
375° Fahrenheit (190° Celsius)
400° Fahrenheit (200° Celsius)

Kitchen Tools

Baking sheet

Blender

Butter knife

Cooking spray

Cooling rack

Cutting board

Ladle

Measuring cups

Measuring spoons

Melon baller

Metal spatula

Microwave-safe bowls

Muffin cups

Muffin pan

Oven mitts

Mixing bowls

Parfait glasses

Paring knife

Pie dish

Plastic spatula

Plastic wrap

Parchment paper

Plate

Rubber spatula

Small drinking glass

Tall drinking glass

Toothpicks

Whisk

Wooden spoon

7

Rise and Shine Smoothies

INGREDIENTS
1 banana
1 1/2 cups strawberries
2 cups low-fat vanilla yogurt
1 cup orange juice
2 cups ice cubes
1/2 cup cereal
(your favorite kind)

TOOLS
Cutting board
Butter knife
Measuring cups
Blender
Drinking glasses

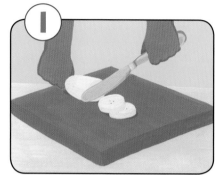

1. Peel and slice the banana with a butter knife.

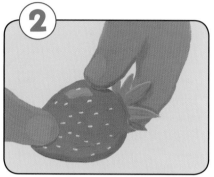

2. Wash the strawberries and pinch off the green stems and leaves.

3. Place the banana, strawberries, yogurt, orange juice, and ice cubes in a blender.

4. Cover and blend on high speed for 30 seconds or until mixture is smooth.

5. Pour into four glasses.

6. Sprinkle a handful of cereal on top of each glass and serve.

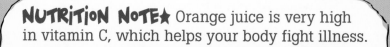

NUTRITION NOTE Orange juice is very high in vitamin C, which helps your body fight illness.

Very Berry Shakes

INGREDIENTS
3/4 cup frozen grape
   juice concentrate
1 cup frozen blueberries
2 cups low-fat vanilla yogurt
1 cup milk
2 cups ice cubes

TOOLS
Measuring cups
Blender
Drinking glasses

1

Let the grape juice concentrate
and frozen blueberries thaw at
room temperature for 10 minutes.

2

Place all of the ingredients into
a blender.

3

Cover and blend on high speed
for 30 seconds or until mixture
is smooth.

4 Pour into four glasses
and serve.

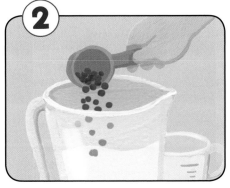

NUTRITION NOTE★ Grape
juice helps keep your heart and
cardiovascular system healthy.

This Recipe Includes
MILK, GRAINS

Breakfast Sundaes

INGREDIENTS

2 cups low-fat yogurt
   (one or more of your
   favorite flavors)
1/3 cup jam
   (your favorite flavor)
1 cup granola
1/4 cup honey

TOOLS

Measuring cups
Measuring spoons
4 parfait glasses or
   tall drinking glasses

1 Spoon 1/4 cup of yogurt into each glass.

2 Add 1 tablespoon of jam.

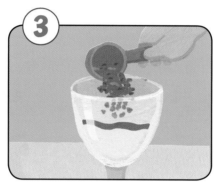

3 Add 2 tablespoons of granola.

4 Drizzle a bit of honey on top.

5 Repeat to build another layer of each ingredient.

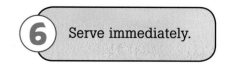

6 Serve immediately.

Easy Cheesy Quiche

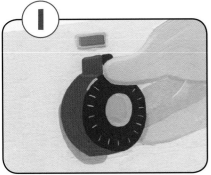

Preheat the oven to 375°.

Pour the eggs, cream, and milk in a medium mixing bowl and whisk together.

Spread the cheese and ham around the bottom of the pie shell.

Pour the egg mixture on top of the cheese.

Ask an adult to bake the quiche for 50 minutes or until a butter knife inserted into the center comes out clean. Let cool for 10 minutes.

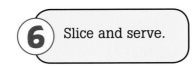

Slice and serve.

INGREDIENTS
5 large eggs
1/2 cup heavy cream
1/2 cup milk
9-inch frozen pie shell
   in a foil pan
1 cup shredded
   cheddar cheese
1 cup cubed deli ham

TOOLS
Measuring cups
Medium mixing bowl
Whisk
Oven mitts
Butter knife

NUTRITION NOTE★ Eggs are high in protein, which helps the body make cells and muscles.

11

This Recipe Includes **FRUITS, MILK, GRAINS, MEAT & BEANS**

Apple 'n' Cheddar Bagel Bites

INGREDIENTS
1 apple
4 bagel halves
4 slices deli ham
4 slices cheddar cheese

TOOLS
Cutting board
Paring knife
Melon baller
Baking sheet
Oven mitts
Cooling rack

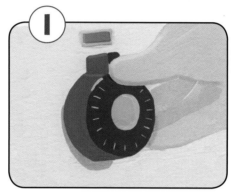

Preheat the oven to 350°.

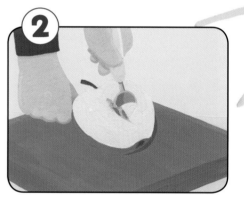

Wash the apple and have an adult cut it in half. Use the melon baller to remove the core.

Have an adult slice the apple into thin wedges.

Place bagel halves on the baking sheet. Put a slice of ham on each bagel half.

FOOD FACT To keep an apple from turning brown after it is cut, rub some lemon juice on it.

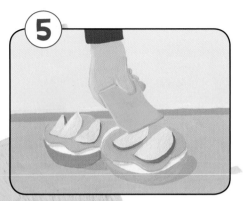

5 Top with a few slices of apple and a slice of cheese.

6 Ask an adult to bake for 8 minutes or until the cheese is melted. Let cool 5 minutes.

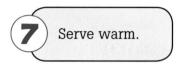

7 Serve warm.

13

This Recipe Includes

MILK, GRAINS, MEAT & BEANS

Microwave Scramble

INGREDIENTS
6 large eggs
2 tablespoons milk
1/2 teaspoon salt
1/2 cup shredded
   cheddar cheese
4 slices toast

TOOLS
Medium microwave-safe bowl
Measuring cups
Measuring spoons
Whisk
Rubber spatula

In a medium microwave-safe bowl, whisk the eggs with the milk and salt.

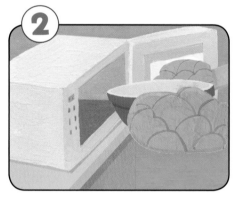

Ask an adult to microwave the eggs for 1 minute.

Stir with the rubber spatula.

Ask an adult to microwave the eggs for 1 minute more.

5

Stir in half of the cheese with the rubber spatula.

6

Ask an adult to microwave the eggs for 45 seconds more.

7

Spoon an equal amount of egg mixture over each piece of toast.

8 Sprinkle with the remaining cheese and serve.

This Recipe Includes
FRUITS, GRAINS

Blueberry Breakfast Pancake

INGREDIENTS

1 tablespoon butter
1 cup fresh blueberries
1/4 cup sugar
3 large eggs
1 cup milk
3/4 cup all-purpose flour
3/4 teaspoon pure
    vanilla extract
2 tablespoons confectioners'
    sugar, optional
Maple syrup, optional

TOOLS

9-inch pie dish
Measuring cups
Measuring spoons
Blender
Oven mitts

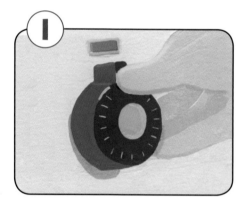

Preheat the oven to 400°.

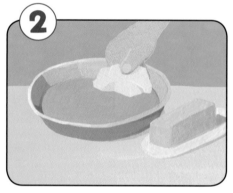

Grease the pie dish with butter.

Wash and drain the blueberries and spread them on the bottom of the pie dish.

Place the sugar, eggs, milk, flour, and vanilla in blender. Cover and blend on low speed for 30 seconds.

5

Pour the batter over the blueberries.

6

Ask an adult to bake the pancake for 30 minutes or until it is puffy and golden. Let cool for 5 minutes.

7 Cut the pancake into wedges and serve with a sprinkle of confectioners' sugar or maple syrup, if desired.

This Recipe Includes
GRAINS

Puffy Popovers

INGREDIENTS
4 large eggs
1 cup milk
3 tablespoons vegetable oil
1 cup all-purpose flour
3/4 teaspoon salt
Butter, optional
Jam, your favorite kind,
    optional

TOOLS
Cooking spray
Muffin pan
Measuring cups
Measuring spoons
Blender
Oven mitts
Toothpicks
Plate

1 Preheat the oven to 400°.

2 Spray the muffin pan with cooking spray.

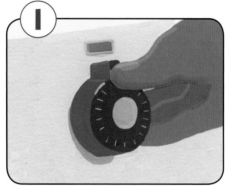

3 Combine the eggs, milk, and oil in blender; cover and blend on medium speed for 10 seconds.

4 Add the flour and salt; cover and blend on low speed for 10 seconds more.

5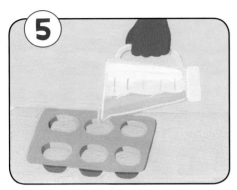

Pour the batter into the muffin cups, filling each cup about three-quarters full.

6

Ask an adult to bake the popovers for 30 minutes or until puffy and golden brown. [Note: Don't open the oven door until the popovers are fully puffed or they might collapse!]

7

Tip the popovers out onto a plate and poke each popover with the toothpick a couple of times to let steam escape.

8 Serve warm with butter and jam, if desired.

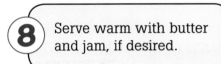

This Recipe Includes

FRUITS, GRAINS

Appley Oatmeal

INGREDIENTS

1 apple
2/3 cup raisins
2 cups rolled oats
1 teaspoon ground
    cinnamon
2 cups apple juice
2 cups water
1/4 cup pure maple syrup

TOOLS

Paring knife
Cutting board
Melon baller
Large microwave-safe bowl
Measuring cups
Measuring spoons
Wooden spoon
Plastic wrap
Oven mitts

Wash the apple and have an adult cut it in half. Use the melon baller to remove the core.

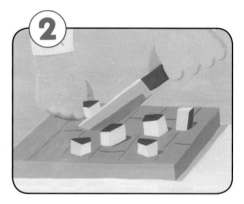

Have an adult cut the apple into pieces.

In a large microwave-safe bowl, stir together the apple, raisins, oats, cinnamon, apple juice, and water.

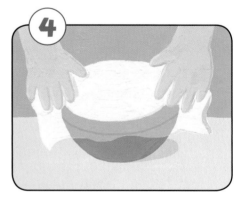

Cover the bowl tightly with plastic wrap.

FOOD FACT★ It takes about 10 gallons of sap from a maple tree to make 1 quart of pure maple syrup.

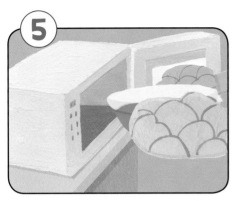

5

Ask an adult to microwave the mixture for 7 minutes or until the apples are soft and the liquid is absorbed.

6

Carefully remove the plastic wrap and stir in the maple syrup.

7 Spoon the oatmeal into bowls and serve.

This Recipe Includes
FRUITS, GRAINS

Surprise! Muffins

INGREDIENTS

6 strawberries
1 banana
2 cups all-purpose flour
1 tablespoon baking powder
1/2 cup sugar
1/2 teaspoon salt
4 tablespoons butter,
    cut into small pieces
2 large eggs
1 cup milk
1 teaspoon pure vanilla
    extract

TOOLS

Muffin pan
Muffin cups
Cutting board
Butter knife
2 large mixing bowls
Whisk
Measuring cups
Measuring spoons
Small microwave-safe bowl
Small ladle
Oven mitts

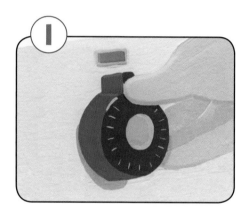

Preheat the oven to 350°.

Line the muffin pan with the muffin cups.

Wash the strawberries and pinch off the green stem and leaves. Peel the banana and cut it into slices.

In a large mixing bowl, whisk the flour with the baking powder, sugar, and salt.

5

Place the butter in a small microwave-safe bowl. Ask an adult to microwave the butter for 40 seconds or until melted.

6

In another large bowl, whisk together the eggs, milk, melted butter, and vanilla until combined.

7

Pour the milk mixture over the flour mixture and whisk until the batter is smooth.

8

Use a small ladle to fill each muffin paper halfway with the batter.

9

Press a strawberry into six of the muffins and a banana slice into the rest. Ask an adult to bake the muffins for 30–35 minutes or until lightly golden. Let muffins cool for 10 minutes.

10 Serve muffins warm or at room temperature.

This Recipe Includes
GRAINS, MILK, MEAT & BEANS

Wide-Eyed Eggs in Toast

INGREDIENTS
4 slices whole wheat bread
4 large eggs
Pinch of salt
Pinch of freshly ground
   black pepper
1/3 cup shredded
   cheddar cheese

TOOLS
Baking sheet
Cooking spray
Small drinking glass
Oven mitts
Plastic spatula

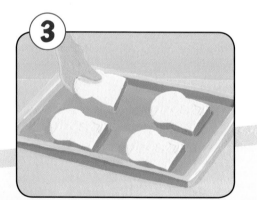

1 Preheat oven to 375°.

2 Spray the baking sheet with cooking spray.

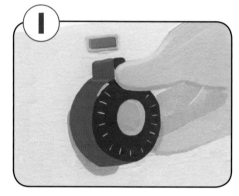

3 Place the bread on the prepared baking sheet.

4 Use the drinking glass to cut a small hole in the center of each piece of bread. Remove the bread circle and discard.

NUTRITION NOTE★ Whole wheat bread is a great source of whole grains. Whole grains contain fiber, vitamins, and minerals. They help prevent heart disease.

5

Fill the hole in each slice of bread by cracking an egg into it.

6

Sprinkle each egg with salt, pepper, and cheese.

7

Ask an adult to bake the toast and eggs for 12 minutes or until the eggs are cooked and the bread is toasted.

8 Remove each piece of toast with a spatula and place on a plate. Serve warm.

This Recipe Includes
MILK, GRAINS

Peanut Butter and Chocolate Chip Scones

INGREDIENTS

3 tablespoons smooth peanut butter
1/2 cup vanilla yogurt
1 1/4 cups biscuit mix
1/4 cup semisweet chocolate chips
1/8 cup flour
1 tablespoon sugar

TOOLS

Measuring cups
Measuring spoons
Large mixing bowl
Wooden spoon
Baking sheet
Cooking spray
Paring knife
Oven mitts

Preheat the oven to 375°.

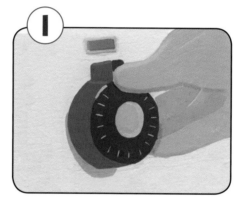

Place the peanut butter and yogurt into a large mixing bowl and stir.

Stir in the biscuit mix and chocolate chips. Spray the baking sheet with cooking spray and transfer the dough to the baking sheet.

Cover your clean hands with flour and pat the dough into a circle. The dough should be about 1 inch thick.

FOOD FACT★ Americans eat enough peanut butter each year to make about 10 billion peanut butter and jelly sandwiches!

5

Sprinkle the dough with sugar.

6

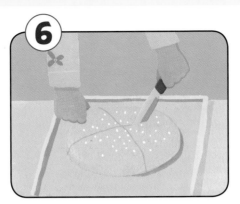

Cut the circle into 8 pie-shaped wedges, separating them slightly.

7

Ask an adult to bake the dough for 20 minutes or until golden brown. Let cool for 10 minutes.

8 Serve warm or at room temperature.

This Recipe Includes

GRAINS, FRUITS, MILK

Getcha-Going Granola

INGREDIENTS

1/3 cup vegetable oil
1/2 cup honey
2 teaspoons pure
 vanilla extract
1/2 cup packed light
 brown sugar
1 1/2 cups chopped nuts and
 seeds, such as walnuts,
 almonds, pecans, and
 sunflower seeds
1/2 cup bran flakes cereal
1 1/2 cups rolled oats
1 cup dried fruit, such as
 raisins, cranberries,
 apricots, or blueberries
Yogurt or milk, optional

TOOLS

Cooking spray
Baking sheet
Large mixing bowl
Whisk
Measuring cups
Measuring spoons
Wooden spoon
Oven mitts

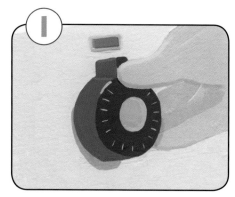

Preheat the oven to 325°.

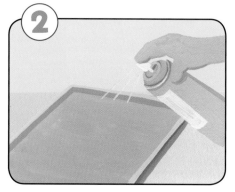

Spray the baking sheet with cooking spray.

In a large bowl, whisk the vegetable oil with the honey, vanilla, and brown sugar.

Stir in the nuts, bran flakes, and oats.

NUTRITION NOTE Nuts contain omega-3 fatty acids, which are good for your heart.

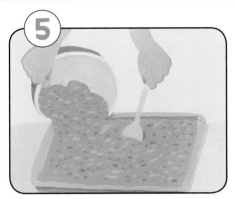

5

Spread the mixture onto the baking sheet.

6

Ask an adult to bake the granola for 45 minutes or until the granola is golden brown. Let cool for 15 minutes.

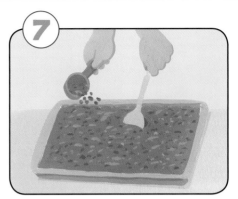

7

Stir in the dried fruit.

8 Serve the granola plain or with yogurt or milk.

This Recipe Includes
GRAINS

Crunchy Munchy French Toast

INGREDIENTS

3 large eggs
1 1/2 cups milk
1 teaspoon vanilla extract
8 slices of toast
3 cups cornflakes cereal,
  crushed into small pieces
Butter, optional
Maple syrup, optional

TOOLS

Baking sheet
Parchment paper
Measuring cups
Measuring spoons
2 large mixing bowls
Whisk
Metal spatula
Oven mitts

Preheat the oven to 400°.

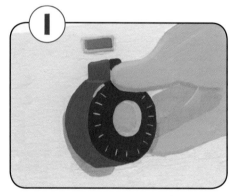

Line a baking sheet with parchment paper.

In a large mixing bowl, whisk the eggs with the milk and vanilla.

Dip both sides of one slice of bread in the egg mixture.

Dip both sides of the egg-moistened bread in the crushed cornflakes.

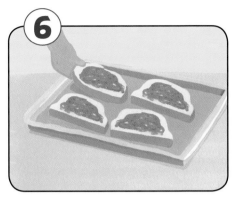

Place on baking sheet. Repeat steps 4–6 with each slice of bread.

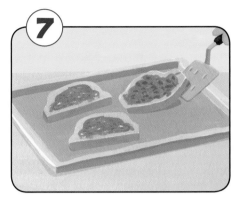

Ask an adult to bake the battered toast for 12 minutes, then flip the toast over with a metal spatula and bake for another 12 minutes or until golden brown.

Place two pieces of French toast on each plate and serve warm with butter and maple syrup, if desired.

31

INDEX

ON THE WEB

FactHound offers a safe, fun way to find Web sites related to topics in this book.
All of the sites on FactHound have been researched by our staff.

1. Visit *www.facthound.com*
2. Type in this special code: 1404839968
3. Click on the FETCH IT button.

Your trusty FactHound will fetch the best sites for you!

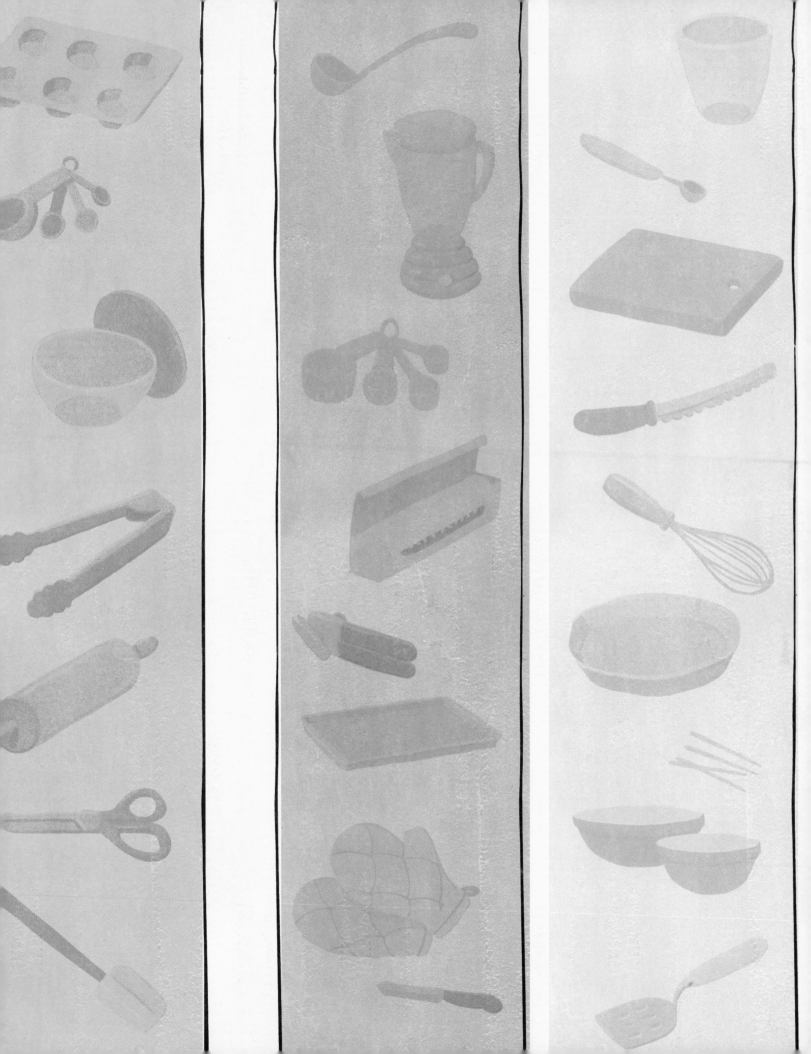

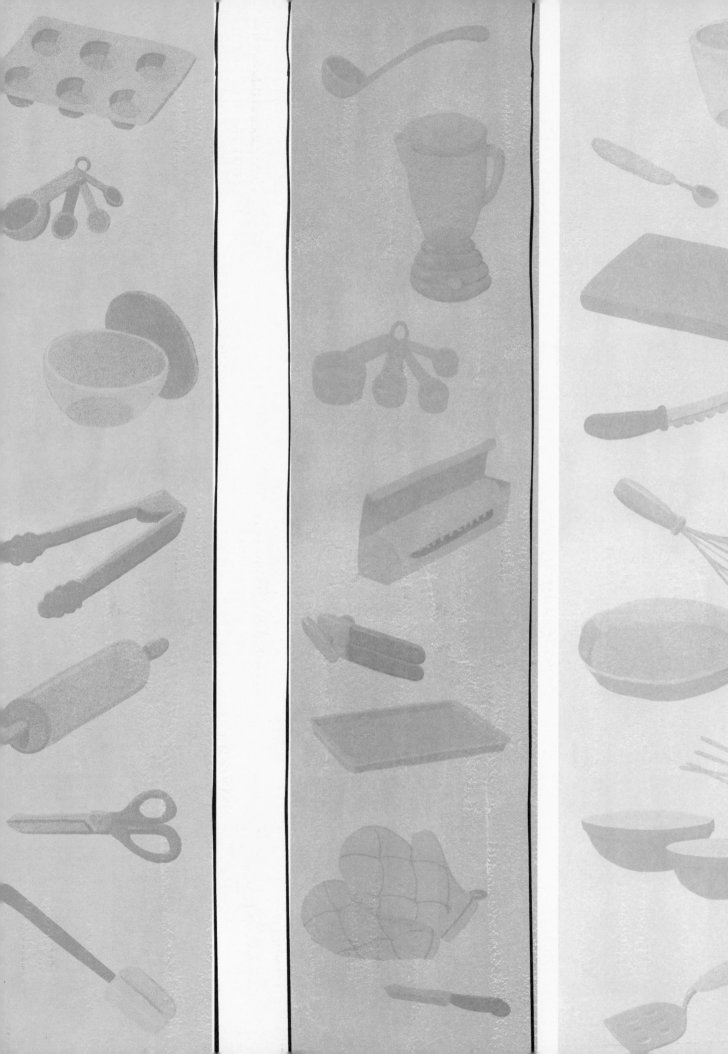